In memory of times when darkness spread,
When truth was twisted, and fears were fed.
It honors the bravery, the courage, the fight,
Those who were lost, and those who stood for what's right.

For my Dad, Karl Stein, Holocaust survivor, whose wisdom I'll always share,
Guiding us to be kind, spreading love and care.
"Stick together, do good," his parting words in my heart still sound,
When we stand united, his legacy can be found.

For my sister, Ariella Stein (Lala), who fought with all her might,
Wrapped in love's web, she knew only love would win her fight.
On the day she left us, her love spread far and wide,
It lives in every breath and brings peace deep inside.

Dear Parents,

As we raise our children, we look for ways to help them skillfully manage life's ups and downs. In "Shalva's Web," you'll find the wisdom of spiders in the inspiring story of Shalva, sharing important lessons for both you and your child. With every reading, you'll deepen your bond and equip yourselves with the tools needed to face challenges, all while embracing courage and creativity. May this story inspire many meaningful moments together.

First Edition - November 2024

Written by Ilana Stein-Attali
Illustrated by Lara Korotenko

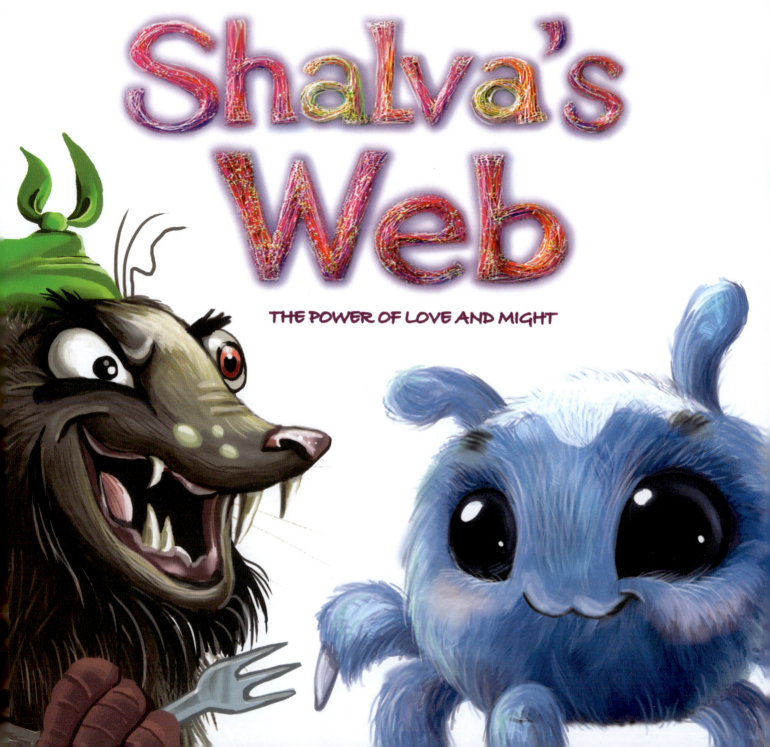

Ilana Stein-Attali   Lara Korotenko

Shalva's Web

THE POWER OF LOVE AND MIGHT

In a mystical land by the Mediterranean Sea,
Where ducks dreamed of being happy and free.
Lived Shalva the spider, spinning webs so bright,
And Bassa the mole, spreading terror with every bite.

While Bassa dreamt of ruling and taking control,
Shalva hoped for friendship with peace as her goal.
As Bassa dug tunnels, hiding treasures with pride,
Shalva spun webs with love and protection inside.

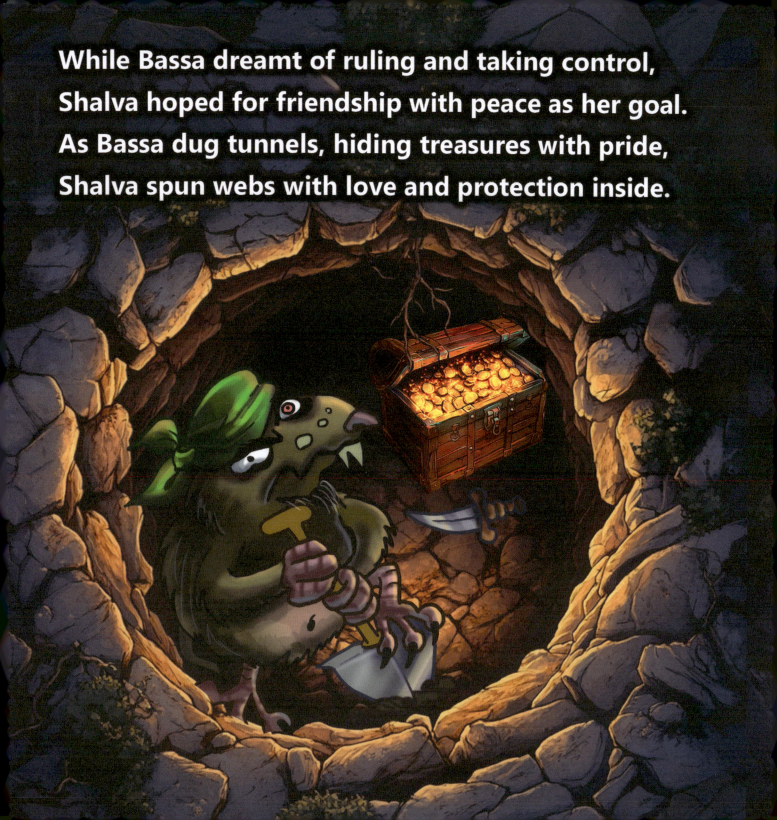

Early one morning as Bassa snuck by,

He spotted happy ducks, dancing, singing

and sleeping under the sky.

"I'll snatch them for my tunnels" he thought,

"that would be yummy."

"They could serve as good company or fill up my tummy."

The ducks were scared, they didn't want to go,
Bassa grabbed them anyway, ignoring their screams of
"No! Stop! No!"
As days turned to months, the ducks grew lost and so alone,
But their families never stopped demanding,
"Bring them home! Bring them home!"

Ignoring their pleas, with a heart cold as stone,
Bassa snarled, "I'm keeping them in this place
that's dark and unknown."
But one day, a fierce storm flooded the tunnels with a roar,
And Bassa, now helpless, began to worry like never before.

Knowing that Shalva cared for each and every duck,
Bassa confessed, "The ducks are here,
                                    and we're all truly stuck."

Though Shalva was determined to rescue and to save,
She was careful to act because she knew
                                    how moles behaved.

Don't you bite me!" Shalva cautioned with a frown.

"I swear, I won't," Bassa replied, "or we both
might drown."

As Shalva came near, Bassa's teeth were on display,
Realizing this intent, she asked, "Why do you act this way?"

"It's just my nature," Bassa chuckled, with delight,
"It's the way that I fight, it's the essence of my might.

This time, Shalva spun a cloak so strong and tight,

That even Bassa's sharpest teeth couldn't make a single bite.

Hooray! Everyone floated home, safe in the sky,

And Bassa, puzzled, asked, "Shalva, you worked

so hard to save them... but why?"

"It's just my nature" Shalva chuckled her eyes
gleaming with delight,
"It's the way that I fight, It's the essence
of my might!"

Let Shalva and her mighty web show us the way,
That our nature is shaped by the choices
we make each day.

When we are brave and stand for what's right,
We discover protection in the web of love and might.

So hold my hand and hug me tight,

It's the love in this web that wins every fight.

My web might be soft and sometimes it breaks, but I can fix it and make it stronger than steel. I'm like a superhero that way! How do you help yourself get stronger when things get tough?

Even if others are mean, I still work to make the world a better place by being helpful and spreading love. That's how I get my superpowers to help me do anything! Can you keep being loving and doing the right thing, even when others aren't kind?

I can make a safe spot for myself anywhere—by the water, on rocks, or even underground! That's my secret for being strong and powerful! Can you be brave and change what you're doing when you need to?

Printed in Great Britain
by Amazon

61017927R00018